HAL LEONARD
TENOR GUITAR METHOD

BY MARK PHILLIPS

T0039804

PLAYBACK+
Speed • Pitch • Balance • Loop

To access audio, visit:
www.halleonard.com/mylibrary
Enter Code
1506-7986-0191-5934

ISBN 978-1-4950-2887-8

HAL•LEONARD®
CORPORATION
7777 W. BLUEMOUND RD. P.O. BOX 13819 MILWAUKEE, WI 53213

In Australia Contact:
Hal Leonard Australia Pty. Ltd.
4 Lentara Court
Cheltenham, Victoria, 3192 Australia
Email: ausadmin@halleonard.com.au

Visit Hal Leonard Online at
www.halleonard.com

CONTENTS

INTRODUCTION

WHO THIS BOOK IS FOR (WHAT WE ASSUME ABOUT YOU)

This book is intended for people who already play guitar or another stringed instrument to some degree. We assume that you know how to hold a guitar, hold a pick, fret notes, pluck the strings (with a pick or your right-hand fingers), and read tablature. To use this book, you don't have to know how to read music because all examples and songs are presented in both standard notation (for those who do read music) and tablature. The tablature numbers, as you know, tell you which frets to play on what string. And you can learn the rhythms by listening to the online audio tracks.

Because the tenor guitar (tuned in 5ths) has a tuning that's different from that of a standard guitar (tuned mostly in 4ths), its fretboard is like "uncharted territory" for guitar players. All the chord forms, scale patterns, and arpeggio shapes you're familiar with don't apply to the tenor guitar. But the tenor guitar has its own unique forms, patterns, and shapes, and it's the intention of this book to make you familiar with them. When you've completed this book, the tenor's fretboard will be well-charted, and you'll most likely have the necessary maps embedded in your memory.

Although standard tuning for tenor guitar is in 5ths (namely, from low to high, C–G–D–A), some people tune a tenor guitar differently. For example, they may tune the strings like the top four strings (that is, the four highest-sounding strings) of a standard guitar. That way, if they already play guitar, they don't have to learn any new fingerings. But because this book is for those who *do* want to learn their way around a (normally tuned) tenor guitar, we use the standard C–G–D–A tuning for all songs and exercises.

A BRIEF HISTORY OF THE TENOR GUITAR

Back in the early 1900s, Dixieland jazz was all the rage, and its primary rhythm instrument was the four-string tenor banjo (which basically strummed chords). But as Dixieland gradually gave way to the kind of jazz we call "swing," ensembles started to want a rhythm instrument that was less strident-sounding than the banjo. Some guitar manufacturers came to the rescue by producing four-string guitars—some the same size as standard guitars and some slightly smaller—that were tuned exactly like the tenor banjo (that is, C–G–D–A). That allowed banjo players to switch to guitar without having to learn any new fingerings. Eventually, among jazz players, the demand for tenor guitars outgrew the demand for tenor banjos. But in the 1930s and '40s, the standard six-string guitar became more popular, and the tenor guitar began to fade. The folk music boom of 1950s and '60s saw renewed interest in the tenor guitar when such artists as Nick Reynolds of the Kingston Trio favored it. Lately, as they look for interesting alternatives to traditional instruments, contemporary musicians have employed tenor guitars not only in folk and jazz, but in blues, Celtic, and ethnic music as well.

HOW THIS BOOK IS ORGANIZED

The best way to learn your way around the tenor guitar fretboard is by playing scales (and scale sequences), arpeggios (and arpeggio sequences), chords, melodies, and solo pieces in several commonly used keys. Each chapter is devoted to a particular key, and for each key, you'll play:

- Basic scales and arpeggios
- A famous song in "strum and sing" style
- A famous song as a single-note melody
- A famous song as a stand-alone solo piece

In addition, Appendix A provides you with fingerings for 48 common chords, and Appendix B relates all the notes on the tenor guitar fretboard to the musical staff (standard notation).

ABOUT THE AUDIO

To access the audio examples that accompany this book, go to **www.halleonard.com/mylibrary** and enter the code found on page 1.

TUNING THE TENOR GUITAR

The tenor guitar is tuned in 5ths: (low to high) C–G–D–A. The lowest string, C, sounds an octave lower than middle C. Note that, when writing music for tenor guitar in standard notation, all notes are written an octave higher than they sound. Put another way, the tenor guitar sounds an octave lower than written (just as a standard guitar does). This means that the lowest open string, C, is written as middle C (one ledger line below the treble staff), but it actually sounds an octave lower. The diagram below shows how to match the open strings of the tenor guitar to a keyboard instrument.

TUNING TO A KEYBOARD

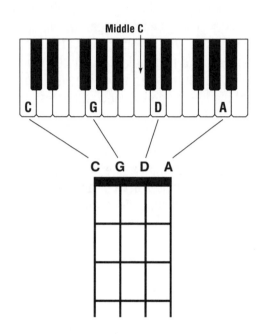

If a keyboard instrument isn't available, you can tune the tenor guitar relative to itself by means of what we call the "seventh fret method." Start by approximating the pitch of the lowest-sounding open string, C, as best you can. Then play that string at the seventh fret to give you the sound of the next-higher open string (the third string, G). Then play the third string at the seventh fret to give the sound of the open second (D) string. Finally, play the second string at the seventh fret to give the sound of the open first string (A). The diagram below should make the process clear.

TUNING THE TENOR GUITAR RELATIVE TO ITSELF

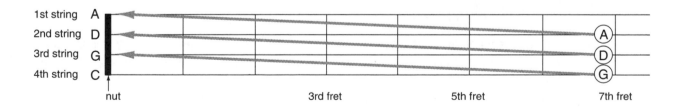

It should be noted that the tenor guitar isn't the only stringed instrument that's tuned in 5ths. The mandolin (with double-string courses rather than single strings) and the violin are tuned in 5ths as well, but they're tuned a 5th higher: (low to high) G–D–A–E. The tenor banjo and the viola are tuned exactly the same as the tenor guitar (C–G–D–A). The cello is also tuned C–G–D–A, but all of the strings sound an octave lower than those of the tenor guitar.

KEY OF C

Let's begin our exploration of the tenor guitar in the key of C. Since this is the pitch of the open fourth string, it's a great place to start.

C MAJOR SCALE

Below is a two-octave C major scale (ascending and descending). The numbers next to the noteheads are left-hand fingerings (1 = index, 2 = middle, 3 = ring, 4 = pinky). Using the first finger for the first fretted note puts you in second position. A *position* on the neck of a fretted instrument is an area of four consecutive frets in which your first finger plays the notes that fall on the lowest of the four frets, your second finger plays the notes that fall on the next-higher fret, and so on. So the position is named after the fret at which your first finger plays. Playing in position minimizes left-hand movement and thus makes fretting easier. By using a combination of open strings and notes in second position, this C major scale is very comfortable to play.

Note that we don't indicate *tempo* (how fast you should play) or *dynamics* (how loudly you should play) for this example. In this book, we provide tempo and dynamic indications for the solo pieces only (the dynamic indication *mf* means to play moderately loud, and *mp* means to play moderately soft). For all scales, arpeggios, and single-note melodies, play at medium volume. Start at a slow tempo, but as you practice, gradually increase your speed with each successive playing.

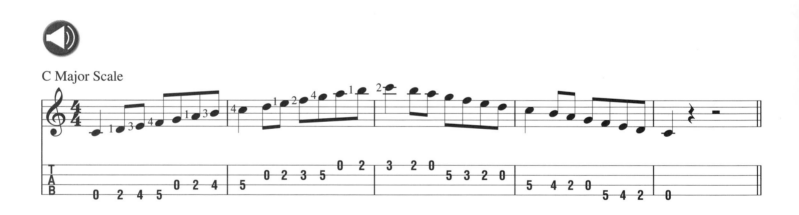

C Major Scale

C MAJOR SCALE SEQUENCE

The following exercise is a *scale sequence* based on the C major scale. In a scale sequence, instead of playing all the notes of the scale in strict order (up or down), you mix things up a bit by taking just a few notes from the scale (say, three or four notes, or even more) and repeating them in a consistent, kind of mathematical pattern—but from a different starting point at each recurrence. For example, in this scale sequence, if you number the scale tones from 1 to 8 (C is 1, D is 2, and so on), you can describe the ascending pattern as 3–1–2–3, 4–2–3–4, 5–3–4–5, and so on. The descending pattern would then be 6–8–7–6, 5–7–6–5, 4–6–5–4, etc. By playing scale sequences, you not only reinforce your knowledge of the scale fingering and of where the scale tones fall on the fretboard, but you also get to feel as if you're playing real music. (In fact, many real songs do employ sequential patterns.) Just as with the previous C major scale example, remain in second position throughout this exercise.

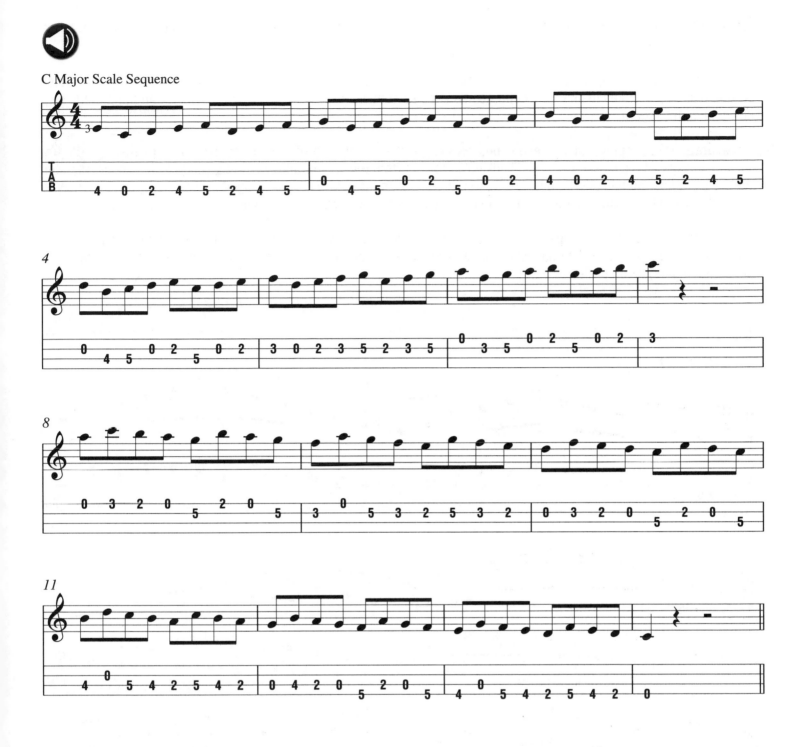

C Major Scale Sequence

ARPEGGIOS IN THE KEY OF C

An *arpeggio* is sometimes called a "broken chord." When you play an arpeggio, you play the notes of a chord one at a time instead of all at once. In the following example, you play arpeggios on all the principal chords in the key of C; namely, C, Dm, Em, F, G, and Am. The chord symbols above the music are for reference—to show you at a glance what chords are being arpeggiated—and are not meant to be played (nevertheless, it would be fine for a chord-playing guitarist or banjoist to add to the festivities by strumming along).

About the chord progression: One of the most famous and popular chord progressions in the world is the progression of "Pachelbel's Canon" (a baroque piece also known as "Canon in D"). In its original key, D major, the repeating, eight-chord progression is D–A–Bm–F♯m–G–D–G–A. In terms of Roman numerals (for theory nerds), this would be I–V–vi–iii–IV–I–IV–V). The progression (or at least a portion of it) has been used in numerous pop songs, including Petula Clark's 1967 hit "Don't Sleep in the Subway" ("You wander around on your own little cloud…"), to cite one example. Because this chord progression is one of the world's most popular, and because it employs a nice variety of major and minor chords, we've used it as the basis of the arpeggio exercises throughout this book. However, note that we've tweaked the ending of the progression a bit in order to work in the otherwise-missing ii chord (the Em chord in the original key of D, or the Dm chord in the example here, in the key of C).

All the notes of the previous C major scale are either open strings or notes in second position. While the arpeggio exercise below is made up of notes mainly in second position, it also contains notes out of position. The left-hand fingerings help guide you in this regard.

In measure 2, use your pinky (still in second position) to play the first string/fifth fret; then (silently) jump up to the 10th fret with your pinky and (again silently) jump back down to the fifth fret with your pinky, putting you back in second position. Note the last fingering numeral in measure 3 (first finger) and in measure 5 (second finger). These are provided simply to get you back into the normal position of the exercise (second position) after having been temporarily out of it.

For the right hand, play this example (and all arpeggio examples in the book) with a pick, using alternate picking (alternate downstrokes and upstrokes). Alternatively, you can use the right-hand fingers (all fingers, all thumb, or a combination of thumb and fingers) if you prefer.

Arpeggios in the Key of C

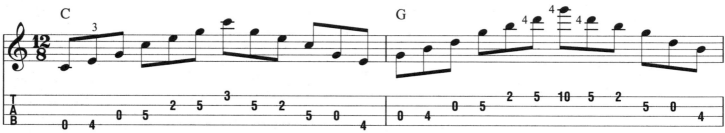

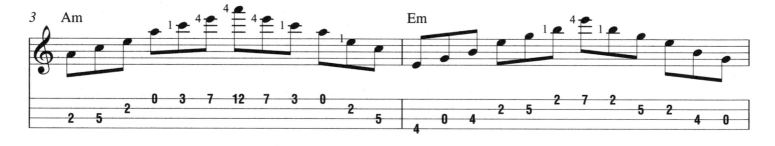

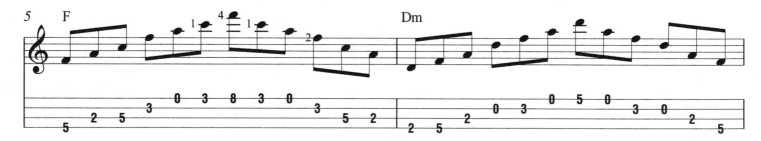

ARPEGGIO SEQUENCE IN THE KEY OF C

Like a scale sequence, an arpeggio sequence lets you mix things up a bit rather than play the notes of each arpeggio in strict ascending or descending order. For the arpeggio sequences, we maintain the modified Pachelbel progression, but within each chord is a sequential pattern. We're playing a zigzag pattern here, moving up two chord tones and down one repeatedly.

The first fingering indication (third finger on the fourth fret) puts you in second position, and, in fact, the entire example can be played using a combination of open strings and notes in second position. Sometimes two consecutive notes are played at the same fret with the same finger on adjacent strings (see the last two notes of measure 1 as an example). To make things easier for your left hand and to provide a smoother sound, rather than fretting each note individually, fret them both at once with a two-string *barre* (i.e., press down both strings at the same time with a single finger). The capital "C" with a vertical line through it (as seen above those last two notes of measure 1) is a notation we've borrowed from classical guitar; it indicates a *partial barre*, which is a barre of anything less than all six strings (in this case, just two strings). The Roman numeral "V" after the barre indication tells you to barre at the fifth fret. Be sure to follow the barre and fingering indications throughout the example.

Arpeggio Sequence in the Key of C

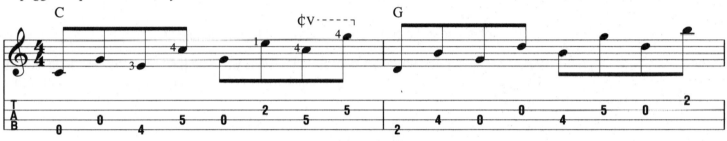

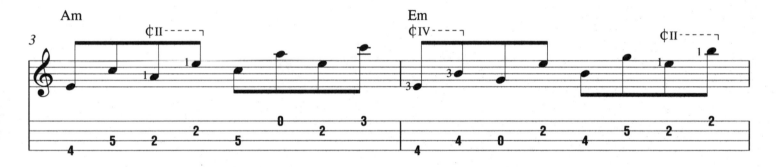

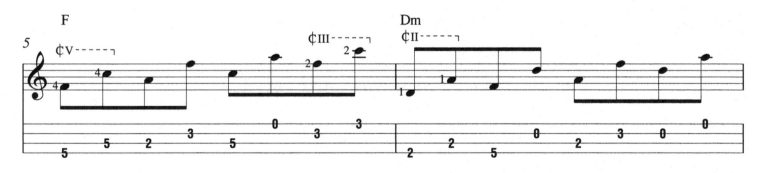

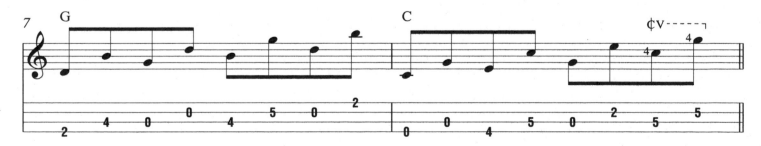

STRUM-AND-SING SONG IN THE KEY OF C

As you know, the chord forms you may know on guitar or banjo don't apply to the tenor guitar, owing to the different tuning. Because the tenor guitar is tuned in 5ths (which is a wider interval than a 4th—the basis of guitar tuning), chords on a tenor guitar have a more open, spread out sound than those on a standard guitar. By strumming and singing well-known songs in various keys (or singing in your mind if you don't like to sing out loud), you can learn basic chords on the tenor banjo. In the song below, which is in the key of C, you learn to play the chords C, D7*, G7, and F. As you work through the book, playing in various keys, you'll learn many more chords. Note that additional chords can be found in "Appendix A: 48 Common Chords."

*Note: Though D7 is not technically found in the key of C, it's a common substitute for Dm in many songs.

In the chord diagrams below:

- The vertical lines represent the strings (the leftmost is the lowest sounding).

- The horizontal lines represent the frets (the top line is the nut, the next lower is the first fret, and so on).

- The dots tell you where (on which strings and at which frets) to place your left-hand fingers.

- The numerals below the strings tell you which finger to use for each note (but feel free to use alternate finger-ings if you find them more comfortable).

- A circle above a string indicates that the string is played open (not fretted).

- A curved line indicates that the notes under the curve are barred (fretted with a single finger).

In the song below, Stephen Foster's "Oh, Susanna," strum the chords indicated as you sing the lyrics. Play the song several times or until you become familiar with the chord shapes. If you're a fingerpicker, feel free to pick (Travis style or any other right-hand style) instead of strum if you so desire.

OH, SUSANNA

    C   D7   G7
I come from Alabama with a banjo on my knee.

      C   G7   C
I'm going to Louisiana, my true love for to see.

     C   D7   G7
It rained all night the day I left; the weather it was dry.

      C   G7   C
The sun so hot I froze to death; Susanna, don't you cry.

F   C   G7
Oh, Susanna, oh, don't you cry for me,

     C   G7   C
For I come from Alabama with a banjo on my knee.

MELODY IN THE KEY OF C

The example below gives you an opportunity to play the melody of an actual song—the early American fiddle classic "Turkey in the Straw." The entire melody falls within second position but contains notes on open strings as well. For the right hand, play as you would on a standard guitar; that is, use a pick and employ alternate picking to whatever extent possible. Start slowly, gradually increasing your speed with each repetition.

 TURKEY IN THE STRAW

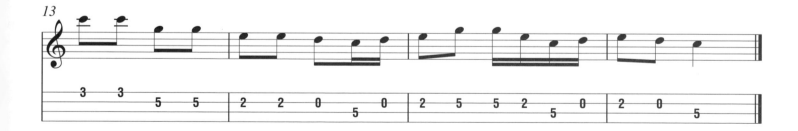

SOLO PIECE IN THE KEY OF C

In a solo piece, instead of playing just chords or melody notes, you combine both (often just little two-note chords, known as *double stops*) to produce a full-sounding, stand-alone arrangement. The solo piece we'll play in the key of C is the classic Christmas carol "The First Noel." While it's possible to play it using a pick, we recommend that you use right-hand fingers.

The curved line joining the first two notes of the piece is a descending slur, telling you to play the second of the two notes as a *pull-off*; that is, the second note of the slur is sounded simply by pulling off the string with the left-hand finger that fretted the first note of the slur (without the right hand striking the string). When playing a pull-off, finger both of the slurred notes at once so that the lower note is already fretted when the higher note is pulled off.

The curved line at the end of the first full measure is an ascending slur, telling you to play the second of the two notes as a *hammer-on*; that is, the second note of the slur is sounded with a left-hand finger that strikes the note (fret) by "hammering down" upon it (again without the right hand striking the string).

The wiggly vertical line you see in front of the chords (the little two-note chords, or double stops) is an arpeggio indication. It tells you to play the notes of the chord not all at the same time (as a chord is normally played), but quickly from low to high. In other words, for each double stop, play the lower note slightly before the higher one, producing a kind of rolling effect.

For simplicity's sake we've notated this piece as a single voice (that is, without separating the melody notes from the accompaniment notes by means of opposing stem directions). But your familiarity with the song allows you to "bring out" the melody by letting all the melody notes ring out as long as possible (and perhaps also by emphasizing them somewhat in terms of volume). For example, in measure 1, allow the low open C note to continue ringing while you play the double stop that follows it. And in measure 3, allow each of the notes on the third string (the melody notes) to continue to ring while you play the higher, offbeat accompaniment notes that follow them. As you work through the book, always bring out the melody of a solo piece by allowing those notes to ring for as long as possible. But also feel free to allow accompaniment notes to ring if it sounds good to you (or if it would be physically awkward to stop them from ringing).

We've indicated some necessary left-hand fingering in the notation. For notes with no fingering given, the fingering should be obvious and/or we encourage you to use whatever fingering feels most comfortable to you. This applies to all solo pieces throughout the book.

THE FIRST NOEL

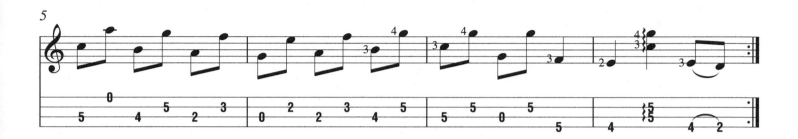

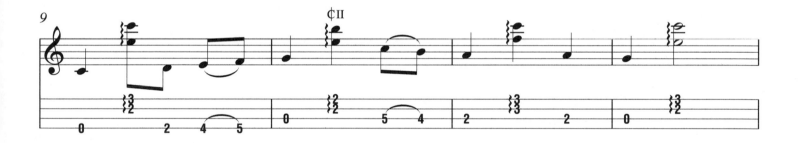

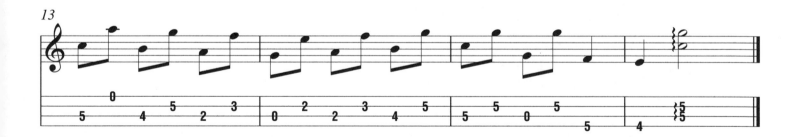

KEY OF G

Next up is the key of G, which also makes use of all the open strings.

G MAJOR SCALE

The two-octave G major scale below starts out nicely in second position, but because it contains several high notes (as high as the 10th fret), you have to make a *position shift* to execute this scale. In measure 2, play the first five notes in second position (or as open strings, as indicated in the tab). Then suddenly but silently move your entire hand up five frets so that you are in seventh position (that is, your index finger is on the seventh fret). Note that, in the notation, we place a horizontal bracket over the notes where the position shift occurs. In measure 3, as the scale descends, play the first three notes in seventh position and then move your entire hand down five frets so that you are back in second position. When you switch positions, the movement should be so subtle (smooth and silent) that a listener wouldn't be able to discern it.

If a scale or arpeggio passage contains only one note higher than the position you're in, you generally move just your pinky up to that higher note (and then back down to its normal position). For a single note that's lower than the current position, you generally move just your first finger down to that note and then back up again. It's only when you have two or more notes out of your original position that you move your entire hand into a new position.

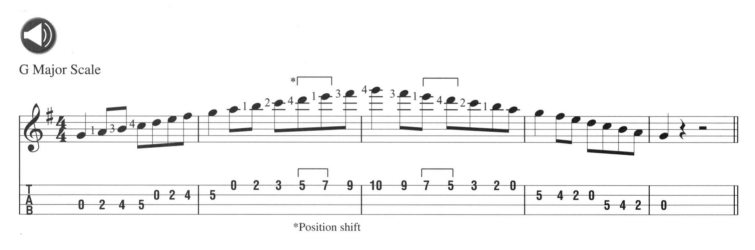

G Major Scale

*Position shift

G MAJOR SCALE SEQUENCE

In the G major scale above, a position shift is indicated in the written notation by means of a bracket. But be aware that, in this book, we show such a bracket only for a position shift in which all the frets of the new position are outside the frets of the original position. When the left hand needs to move only a fret or two from the original position, or when just a single finger is involved in executing an out-of-position note, we indicate that merely with normal left-hand fingering numerals.

Interestingly, when the notes you play force you to move out of position, sometimes you genuinely change position, as in measures 5–7 of the next example, where you move from second position to third, then to fifth, and then to seventh. Other times, a note out of position feels more like an extension (a widening) of the original position, as in measure 15, where you "extend" second position upward by one fret as you grab the note at the sixth fret (fourth string) with your pinky.

G Major Scale Sequence

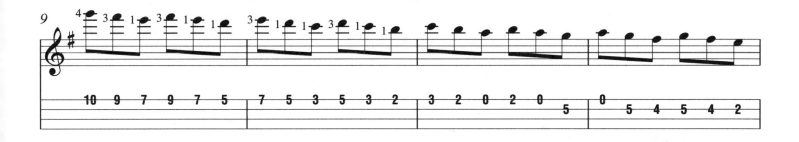

ARPEGGIOS IN THE KEY OF G

The arpeggio example below uses the same modified Pachelbel progression as before, but now we're in the key of G, yielding arpeggios of the chords G, Am, Bm, C, D, and Em (though not in that order). Be sure to follow the notations for left-hand fingerings and position shifts.

Arpeggios in the Key of G

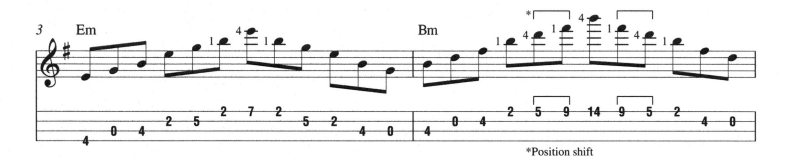

*Position shift

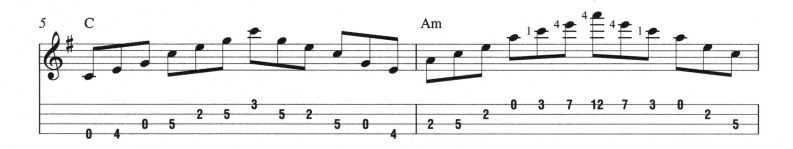

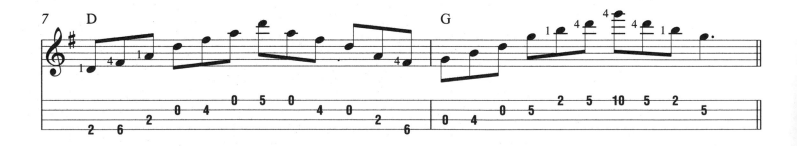

ARPEGGIO SEQUENCE IN THE KEY OF G

In this arpeggio sequence, again based on the modified Pachelbel progression, the repeating pattern consists of an ascent of an octave followed by two descents to consecutive chord tones. Most of the notes are in second position, but follow the fingering indications for notes out of position.

Arpeggio Sequence in the Key of G

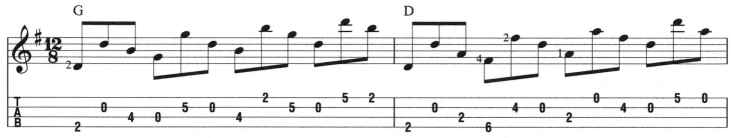

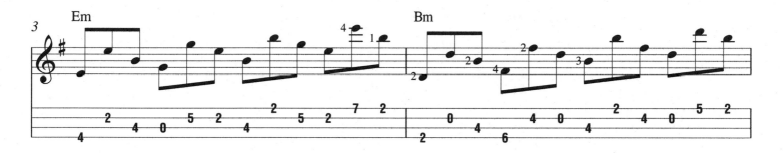

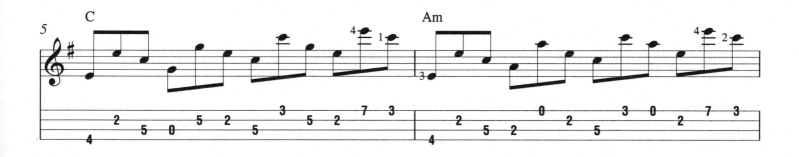

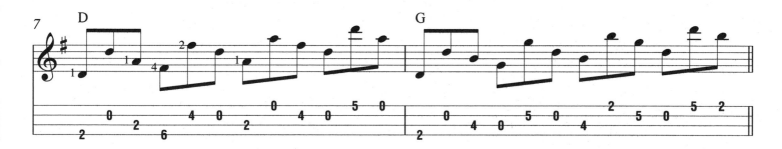

STRUM-AND-SING SONG IN THE KEY OF G

This song, the American spiritual "Swing Low, Sweet Chariot," uses the same C and D7 chords you played in "Oh, Susanna" and introduces two new chords: G and Am7.

 SWING LOW, SWEET CHARIOT

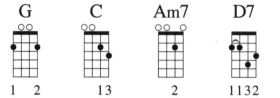

 G   C G   Am7   D7
Swing low, sweet chariot, coming for to carry me home.

 G   C G   D7   G
Swing low, sweet chariot, coming for to carry me home.

 G   C   G   Am7   D7
I looked over Jordan, and what did I see coming for to carry me home?

 G   C   G   D7   G
A band of angels coming after me, coming for to carry me home.

MELODY IN THE KEY OF G

The traditional Irish jig "The Irish Washerwoman" falls nicely in second position in the key of G, but watch for a brief movement to third position (extended upward a fret for the seventh-fret note) in measure 4. For the right hand, use a pick and employ alternate picking.

 THE IRISH WASHERWOMAN

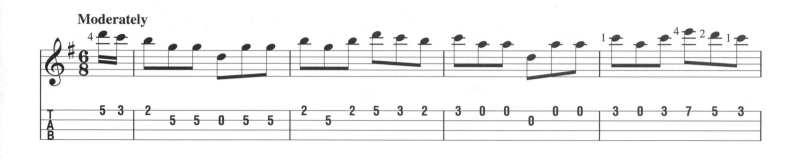

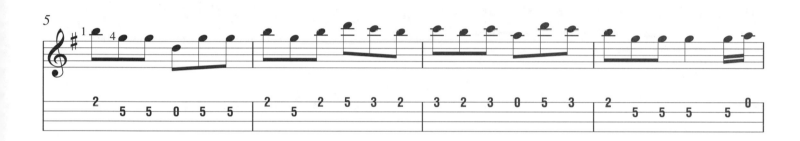

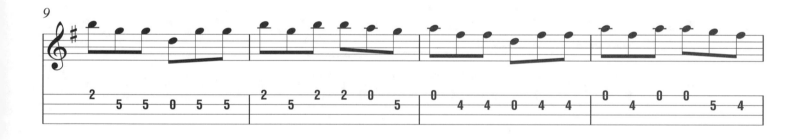

SOLO PIECE IN THE KEY OF G

Beethoven's "Ode to Joy" is a tune famously heard in his Ninth Symphony, but it's sometimes sung with the English lyrics "Bells are ringing, hearts are singing…" As with "The First Noel," in the notation we keep things simple by not separating the melody notes from the accompaniment notes, but again, your familiarity with the tune allows you to bring out the melody. Specifically, play the notes of the melody (mainly the notes that fall on the beats and on the lower strings) with your right-hand thumb and allow them to ring even as you play the accompaniment notes that follow them. The accompaniment notes are mainly the offbeat notes on the higher strings, played here with your right-hand index and middle fingers.

In measures 10 and 11, you see notes that are slurred but with a slanted line under the slur. This indicates a *slurred slide*. Play the first of the two slurred notes normally and then produce the sound of the second note by sliding your finger (the one that played the first note—in this case, your third finger) to the fret of the second note, causing the pitch of that fret to sound (without striking the string with your right hand). For notes with no left-hand fingering indication, use whatever fingering feels comfortable to you if the fingering isn't immediately obvious.

 ODE TO JOY

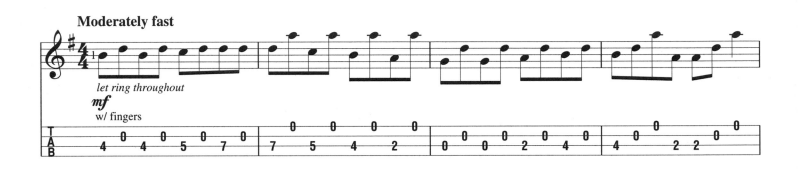

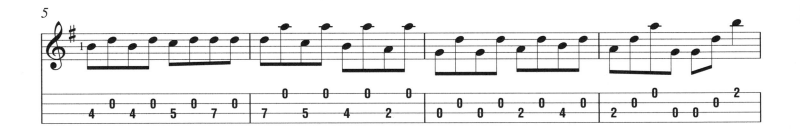

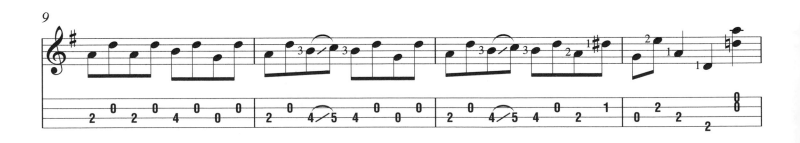

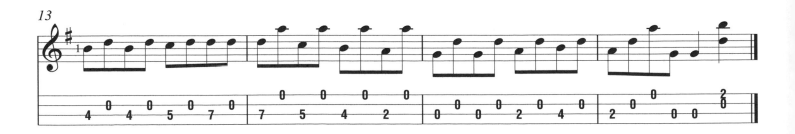

KEY OF F

The key of F major has one flat (B♭). We still make use of all the open strings in this key, but we also have our first note on fret 1, which is a B♭ on string 1.

F MAJOR SCALE

Like the C major and G major scales, the F major scale falls mainly in second position. But watch for a move to first position on string 1. This is followed by a shift to fifth position, another shift back to first position, and finally a return to second position.

F Major Scale

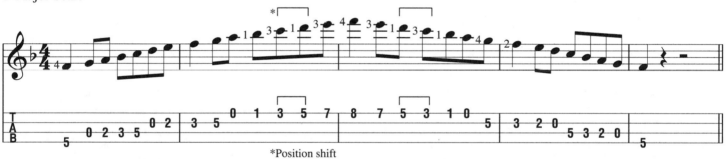

*Position shift

F MAJOR SCALE SEQUENCE

The F major scale sequence below contains several position shifts, so pay careful attention to the fingerings suggested. Concerning the four-note sequence pattern itself, you see that, in the ascending half of the example (measures 1–6), three downward steps are followed by a downward jump of a 3rd (a distance equal to two steps). To describe it mathematically in terms of scale degrees, it would be 5–4–3–1, 6–5–4–2, and so on. In the descending half (measures 7–12), the notes of the repeating figure move in the opposite direction: 4–5–6–8, 3–4–5–7, and so on.

F Major Scale Sequence

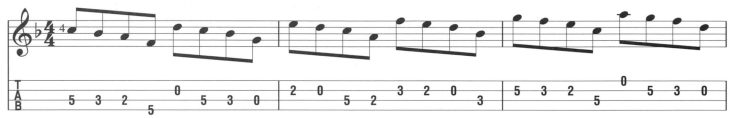

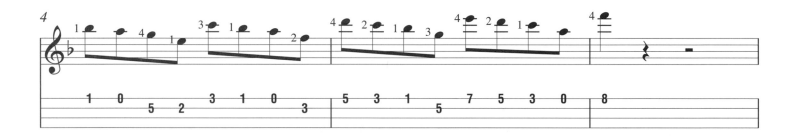

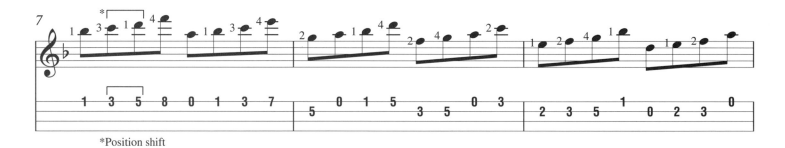

*Position shift

ARPEGGIOS IN THE KEY OF F

In the key of F, the modified Pachelbel progression yields the chords F, Gm, Am, B♭, C, and Dm. Again, watch the fingerings to guide you through the position changes as you arpeggiate the chords in this example.

Arpeggios in the Key of F

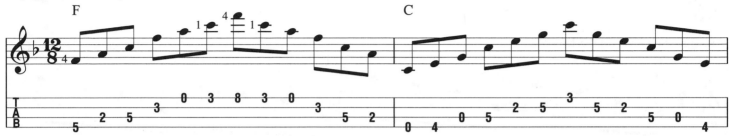

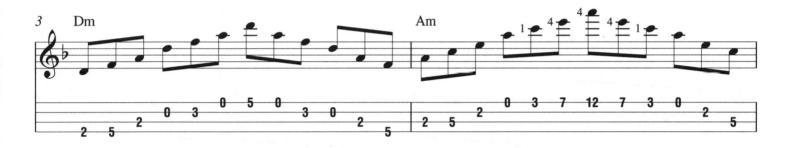

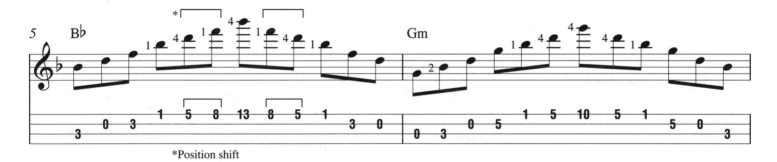

*Position shift

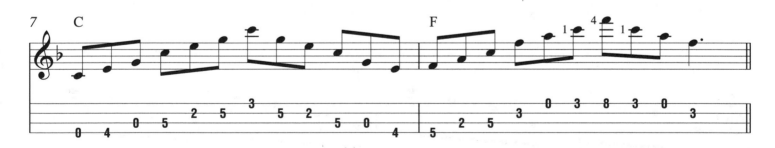

ARPEGGIO SEQUENCE IN THE KEY OF F

This F major arpeggio sequence falls mostly in second position, but, as you see from the fingering indications, you occasionally move down to first position (end of measure 5) or "extend" second position an extra fret downward to grab a note at the first fret (end of measure 6). As with the C major arpeggio sequence, watch for places where you play consecutive notes on adjacent strings at the same fret. Finger these pairs as small (two-string) barres to make the playing easier and the sound smoother.

Arpeggio Sequence in the Key of F

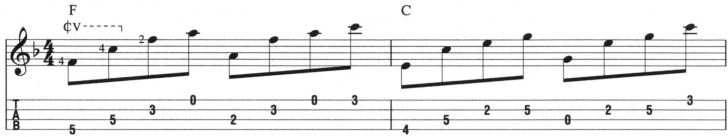

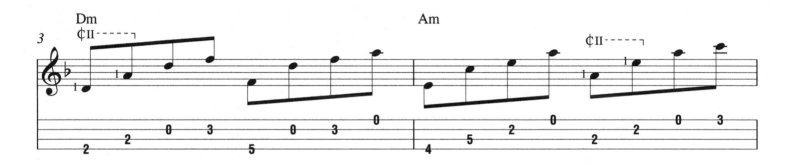

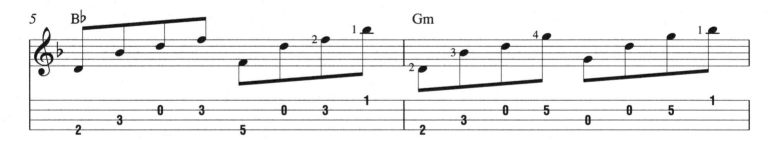

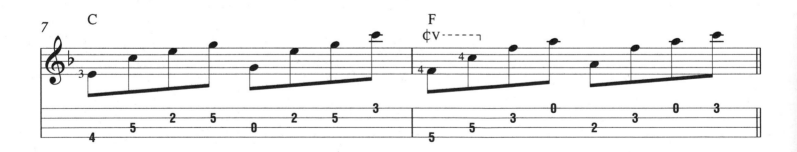

STRUM-AND-SING SONG IN THE KEY OF F

The cowboy song "Home on the Range" uses the same F and G7 chords you played in "Oh, Susanna" and introduces three new ones: Bb, C7, and Bbm.

 HOME ON THE RANGE

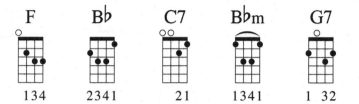

    F   Bb   F   C7

Oh, give me a home where the buffalo roam, where the deer and the antelope play,

    F   Bb   Bbm   F   C7   F

Where seldom is heard a discouraging word and the skies are not cloudy all day.

F   C7   F   G7   C7

Home, home on the range, where the deer and the antelope play,

    F   Bb   Bbm   F   C7   F

Where seldom is heard a discouraging word and the skies are not cloudy all day.

MELODY IN THE KEY OF F

Johann Sebastian Bach's "Jesu, Joy of Man's Desiring" (originally from his Cantata 147) is often performed at wedding ceremonies. Numerous classical artists have recorded it, but the piece crossed over to the popular realm as well after such artists as Amy Grant, Olivia Newton-John, and John Tesh recorded it. As presented here in the key of F (a step lower than Bach's original key of G), the melody should pose no difficulties at all, as its notes are found entirely in second position and on open strings. Use a pick and employ alternate picking as much as possible.

 JESU, JOY OF MAN'S DESIRING

SOLO PIECE IN THE KEY OF F

"Danny Boy" is a famous Celtic song based on the Irish tune "Londonderry Air." Play the melody with your right-hand thumb and play the little chords between the melody notes with the fingers. As before, allow the melody notes to ring out as long as possible (even as you play chords on higher strings above them). Remember that the wavy vertical lines before the chords indicate that they are quickly *arpeggiated* (that is, you roll them quickly from low to high). Note the fingerings and barre indications. You'll see that sometimes you can shift positions by a great number of frets by taking advantage of an open string that occurs between the passages of the two positions in question. For example, at the end of measure 8, as you play the open second string, you silently move your left hand from fifth position to ninth. Other times a simple slide gets you from one position to another (see measures 8–9); still other times you must (silently) move your whole hand into a new position without the help of an open string or a slide (measure 2–3).

DANNY BOY

KEY OF D

In the key of D, we have three open strings available (strings 3, 2, and 1), but the fourth string, open C, is not diatonic to the D major scale. We have to make this a C# note at fret 1 in order to stay within the key. (That's not to say, of course, that we'll never play a C note in a song that's in D; it's just that it's not found in the D major scale.)

D MAJOR SCALE

This two-octave D major scale falls mostly in second position, but you occasionally "extend" second position upward by a fret in order to grab those sixth-fret notes on the fourth and third strings.

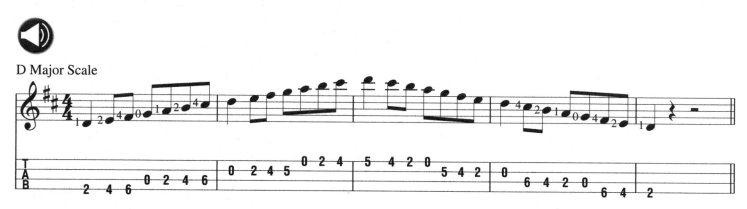

D MAJOR SCALE SEQUENCE

This D major scale sequence consists of a simple three-note figure in which the first and last note of each group are the same and the middle note is a step below. As usual, the fingerings guide you through any necessary position changes.

ARPEGGIOS IN THE KEY OF D

The modified Pachelbel progression is here in Pachelbel's original key of D, yielding the chords D, Em, F#m, G, A, and Bm. The fingerings guide you through the necessary position changes as you arpeggiate these chords.

Arpeggios in the Key of D

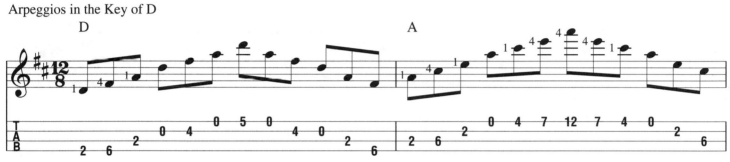

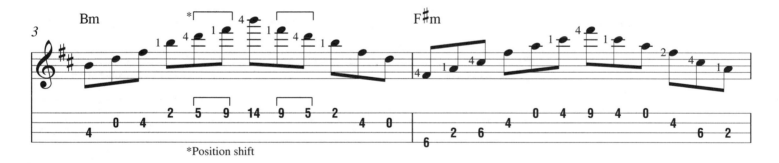

*Position shift

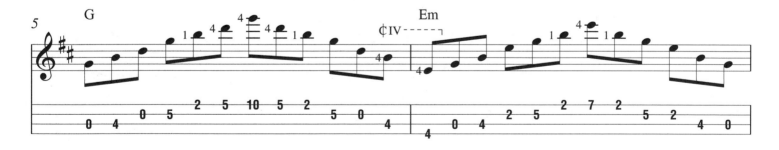

ARPEGGIO SEQUENCE IN THE KEY OF D

The four-note pattern of this arpeggio sequence consists of an ascent to the nearest chord tone, another ascent that skips over one chord tone, and then a descent to the nearest chord tone. As usual, barre consecutive notes on adjacent strings that you play at the same fret. The fingerings guide you through any necessary position extensions and shifts.

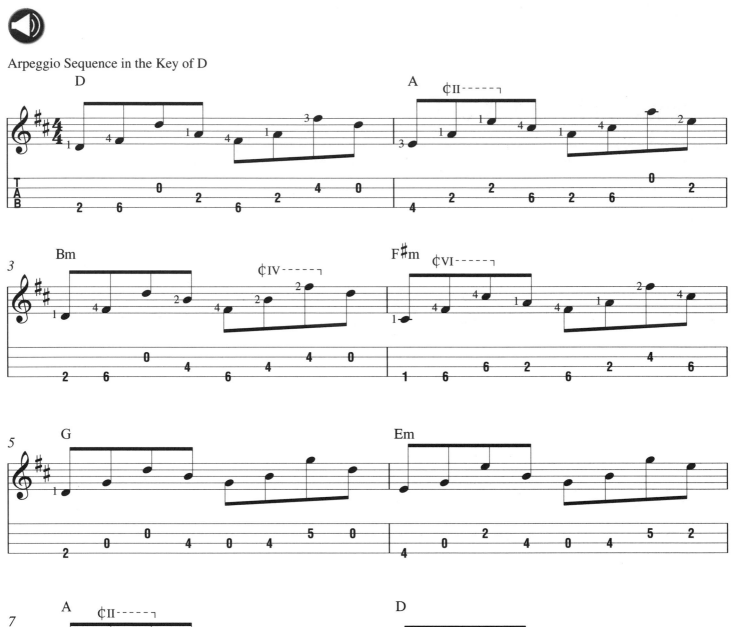

Arpeggio Sequence in the Key of D

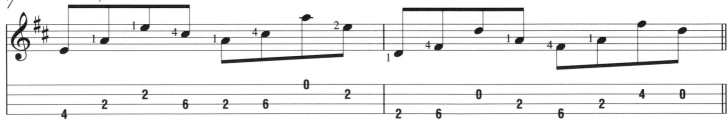

STRUM-AND-SING SONG IN THE KEY OF D

The popular Christmas carol "We Wish You a Merry Christmas" employs a variety of chords: three major chords, two minor chords, and three seventh chords. Note that, in the chord diagrams below for the E7 and F♯7 chords, the first finger plays not at the first fret, but at the fret indicated to the right of the diagram.

 WE WISH YOU A MERRY CHRISTMAS

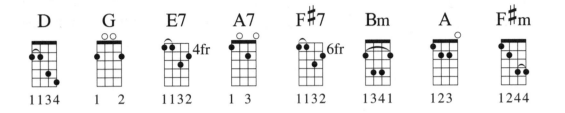

      D   G
We wish you a Merry Christmas,

      E7   A7
We wish you a Merry Christmas,

    F♯7   Bm   G   A7 D
We wish you a Merry Christmas and a Happy New Year.

     Bm   A   E7   A
Good tidings to you, wherever you are.

      D   F♯m   G   A7 D
Good tidings for Christmas and a Happy New Year.

MELODY IN THE KEY OF D

The well-known American fiddle song "Arkansas Traveler" falls entirely in second position (but with open strings employed as well) when played on tenor guitar in the key of D, so this one should present no problems. Use alternate picking as much as possible.

 ARKANSAS TRAVELER

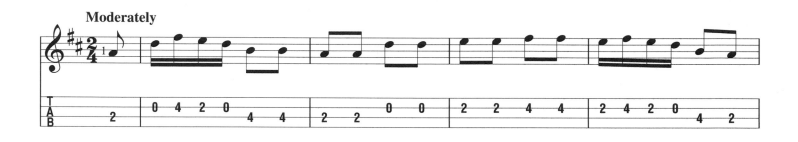

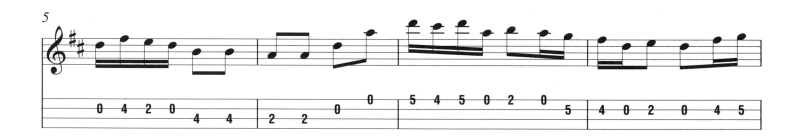

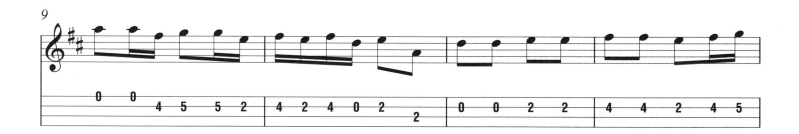

SOLO PIECE IN THE KEY OF D

The traditional American folk song "Shenandoah" (sometimes called "Oh Shenandoah" or "Across the Wide Missouri") has been recorded by an extremely wide range of artists (both folk and non-folk), including Harry Belafonte, Glen Campbell, Bing Crosby, Bob Dylan, Judy Garland, Arlo Guthrie, the Kingston Trio, Van Morrison, Pete Seeger, and Bruce Springsteen.

As with all the solo pieces in this book, bring out the melody; that is, emphasize the melody notes and let them ring as long as possible (over or under any accompaniment notes that occur on other strings). The circled numbers in measure 1 are string numbers; the tab there also indicates that the repeated D melody notes are not all played on the same string. A partial descending slur (see measure 3, for example) indicates that the note following the slur is to be pulled off from the last note played on that string (even though notes on other strings occur between them). In the case of measure 3, because the first note is a melody note, it continues to ring (and is held down) over the next two open string notes. Then, the fourth note of the measure is pulled off from the measure's first note (a pull-off from the second fret of the first string to the open first string). Left-hand fingerings are provided here for the first two notes only. Afterward, if not immediately obvious, use whatever fingering feels comfortable.

 SHENANDOAH

KEY OF A MINOR

The key of A minor should feel familiar to you if you've already worked through the C major chapter.

A MINOR SCALE

The A minor scale contains the same notes as the C major scale, with the only difference being that the C major scale starts from a C note and the A minor scale starts from an A note. Major and minor keys whose scales contain the same pitches are said to be *relative* to one another. So, A minor is the *relative minor* of C major, and C major is the *relative major* of A minor.

Whereas there is only one major scale (the scale that gives the familiar "do re mi fa sol la ti do" sound), there are three different forms of the minor scale. A scale like the one below, which uses the same notes as its relative major, is known as the *natural minor* scale. In A minor, this would be the notes A, B, C, D, E, F, and G. The *harmonic minor* scale is the same except that the 7th degree is raised a half step: A harmonic minor is spelled A–B–C–D–E–F–G♯. The *melodic minor* scale, in its ascending form, is the same as the natural minor except that both the 6th and 7th degrees are raised a half step. But in its descending form, it's identical to the natural minor, with both the 6th and 7th degrees not raised. So the ascending A melodic minor scale is spelled A–B–C–D–E–F♯–G♯, and the descending is the same as A natural minor. For simplicity's sake, in this book we'll base all minor scales and minor scale sequences on the natural minor scale only. However, in the songs you play—whether "strum and sing" songs, single-note melodies, or stand-alone solo pieces—you do encounter some tones from the other forms of the minor scale (that is, you encounter some raised 6th and 7th degrees). Note that, in playing the examples and songs, you don't need to concern yourself with these details; simply read the music as indicated (whether standard notation or tab) as usual.

This two-octave A minor scale begins in second position and moves to seventh position for the higher notes (but with the pinky silently jumping out of seventh position, from the 10th fret to the 12th, for the very highest note of the scale).

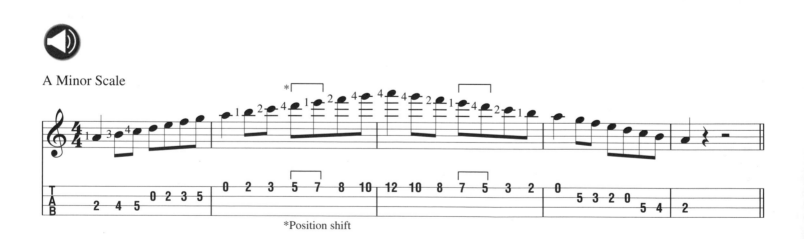

A Minor Scale

*Position shift

A MINOR SCALE SEQUENCE

The ascending half of this A minor scale sequence has the scale degree pattern 3–2–1–3, 4–3–2–4, and so on; the descending half has the opposite: 6–7–8–6, 5–6–7–5, and so on. The lower notes fall nicely in second position. For the higher notes, position changes are required, and these are achieved by numerous one-fret moves up (with the pinky) or down (with the first finger), as indicated by the fingering.

A Minor Scale Sequence

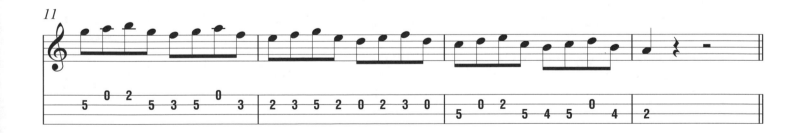

ARPEGGIOS IN THE KEY OF A MINOR

For the arpeggios you played in major keys, we employed what we call the "modified Pachelbel progression" (based on the famous progression of his "Canon in D"). No such "world famous" progression exists for minor keys, but for utility's sake, we imagine what would have happened if Pachelbel had been in a "minor key" mood when he composed his "Canon," and we get the fictional "Canon in D Minor," in which the major key chords I–V–vi–iii–IV–I–IV–V (D–A–Bm–F♯m–G–D–G–A) become the minor key chords i–v–♭VI–♭III–iv–i–iv–v (Dm–Am–B♭–F–Gm–Dm–Gm–Am). But again, we tweak the ending of the progression to incorporate the otherwise missing ♭VII chord (C). So, what we call the "modified minor Pachelbel progession," in the key of D minor, is Dm–Am–B♭–F–Gm–B♭–C–Dm. This progression is suitable for the minor key arpeggio examples in this book because, like its major key counterpart, it's satisfying in structure and it uses a nice variety of chords. Transposing the modified minor Pachelbel progression to the key of A minor, for the sake of this chapter, we get Am–Em–F–C–Dm–F–G–Am, and these are the chords you arpeggiate in the example below.

Most of the example falls in second position, but as usual, the left-hand fingerings guide you through the position changes.

Arpeggios in the Key of A Minor

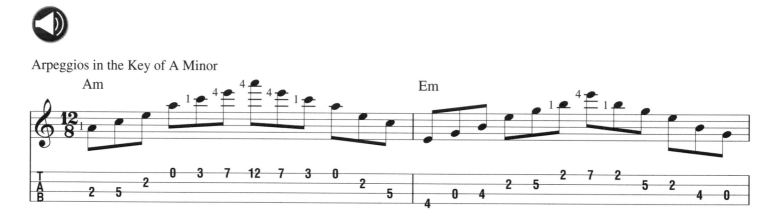

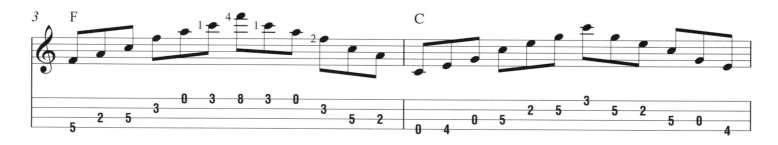

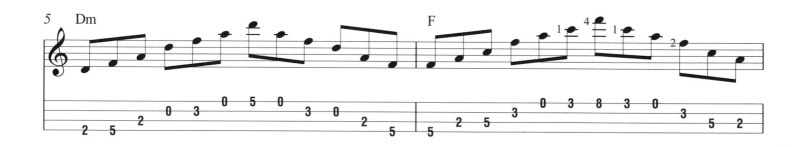

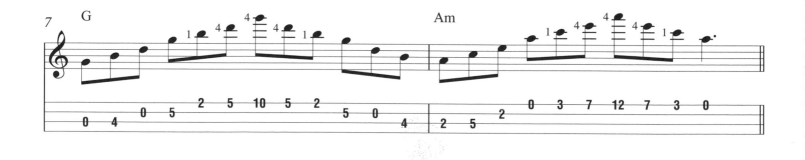

ARPEGGIO SEQUENCE IN THE KEY OF A MINOR

Just as the major key arpeggio sequences are based on the modified Pachelbel progression, the minor key arpeggio sequences in this book are based on the modified minor Pachelbel progression. All the fretted notes of this example are between the second and fifth frets, so your left hand stays in second position throughout; but watch for the little barres you use when the same finger plays consecutive notes on adjacent strings at the same fret.

Arpeggio Sequence in the Key of A Minor

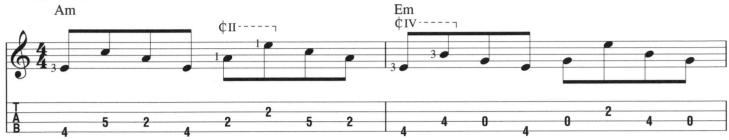

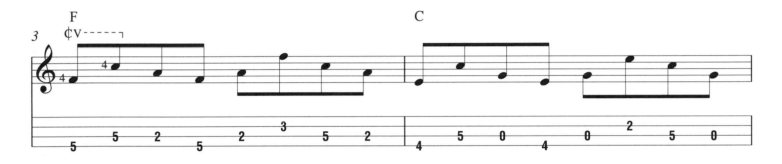

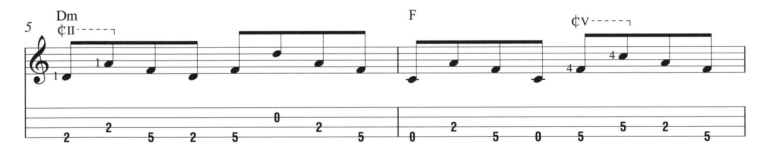

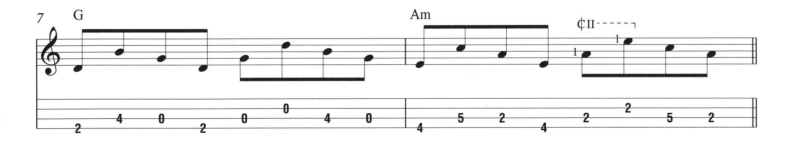

STRUM-AND-SING SONG IN THE KEY OF A MINOR

The traditional folk song "House of the Rising Sun" was a major hit in 1964 for the English rock group the Animals. Three of the song's chords are familiar already: C, D, and F; two others are new: Am and E.

A note for theory nerds: The D chord contains an F# note, and the E chord contains a G# note. These can be seen, respectively, as the raised 6th and 7th notes of the ascending form of the A melodic minor scale.

 HOUSE OF THE RISING SUN

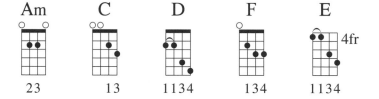

       Am C   D   F   Am   C   E
There is a house in New Orleans they call the Rising Sun,

          Am   C   D   F   Am   E   Am
And it's been the ruin of many a poor boy, and God, I know I'm one.

      Am   C   D   F Am   C   E
My mother was a tailor; she sewed my new blue jeans.

      Am   C   D   F Am   E   Am
My father was a gambling man down in New Orleans.

MELODY IN THE KEY OF A MINOR

If you don't recognize Norwegian composer Edvard Grieg's "In the Hall of the Mountain King" by name, you'll recognize it when you hear it, as it has been used in numerous movies, TV commercials, and video games. The melody is based on the A minor scale but incorporates several tones outside the scale as well.

Note that each four-measure section is repeated. The final four-bar section contains different endings; play measures 9–12 the first time, but 9, 10, 11, and 13 the second time. As usual, follow the fingerings to guide you through the position changes and employ alternate picking.

IN THE HALL OF THE MOUNTAIN KING

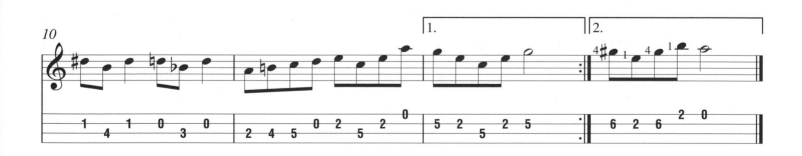

SOLO PIECE IN THE KEY OF A MINOR

The melody of the traditional English folk song "Greensleeves" is the same as that of the classic Christmas carol "What Child Is This?" In this arrangement, most of the melody notes that fall on the strong beats are double stops, with the lower notes played by the right-hand thumb and the upper notes played by the fingers. (All of the single notes are played by the fingers.) There are a number of ways the left hand can finger this piece, so use whatever feels comfortable to you. Note that, as with "House of the Rising Sun," the F♯ and G♯ notes you play are derived from the A melodic minor scale.

GREENSLEEVES

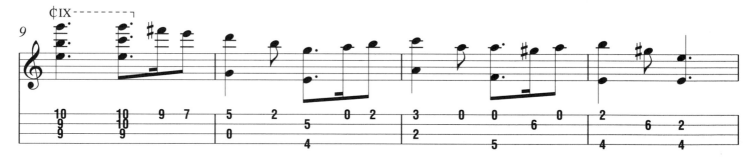

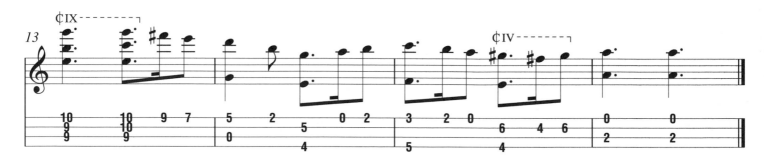

KEY OF E MINOR

If you've worked through the key of G major chapter already, the key of E minor will be a breeze.

E MINOR SCALE

The key of E minor is the relative minor of the key of G major, so the E natural minor scale uses the same notes as the G major scale. (Of course, now we're starting and ending on the note E instead of the note G.) We present some alternate fingerings for a few spots in this scale. Using the lower fingerings (numbers not in parentheses), you play the scale in second position with extensions of the position for the notes at the fourth string/sixth fret and first string/seventh fret. Using the alternate fingerings (numbers in parentheses), you play the first two notes and the last two notes in third position. For the notes on the first string, you move from second position to fifth position and then back again. Use whichever fingering feels more comfortable to you.

E Minor Scale

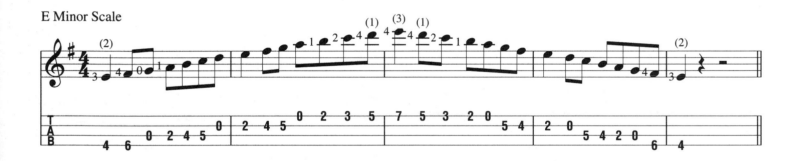

E MINOR SCALE SEQUENCE

This scale sequence is based on a very simple pattern of three stepwise descending notes, with each repetition beginning a step higher than the previous. Of course, in the second half of the example, the situation is reversed. The notes are mainly located in second position (or on open strings), but, as usual, watch the fingerings for position extensions or shifts.

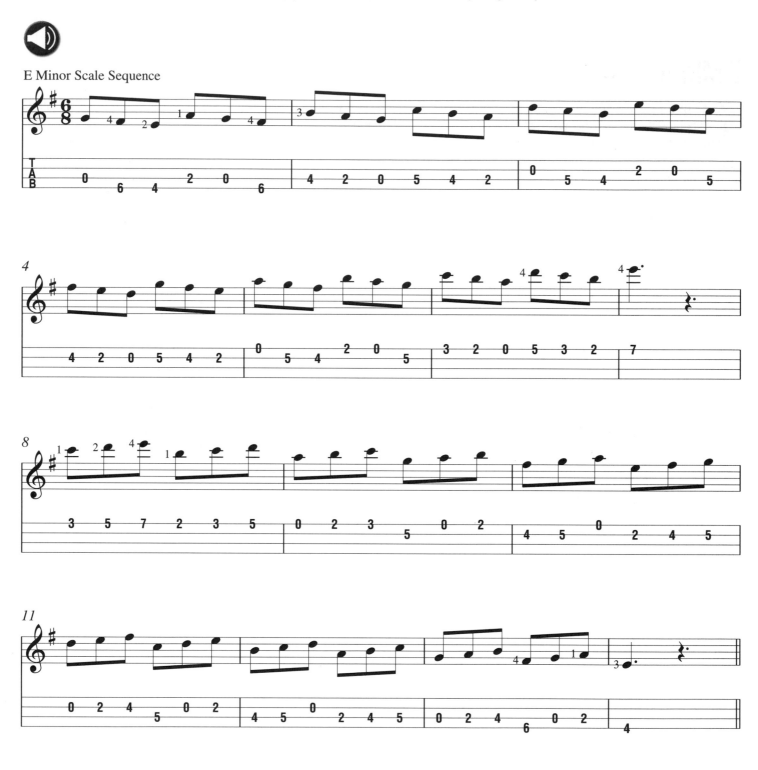

E Minor Scale Sequence

ARPEGGIOS IN THE KEY OF E MINOR

Transposing the modified minor Pachelbel progression to the key of E minor yields the chords Em, G, Am, Bm, C, and D. These are arpeggiated (though not in that order) in the example below, played mainly in second position, with a few position extensions and shifts, as indicated by the fingering.

Arpeggios in the Key of E Minor

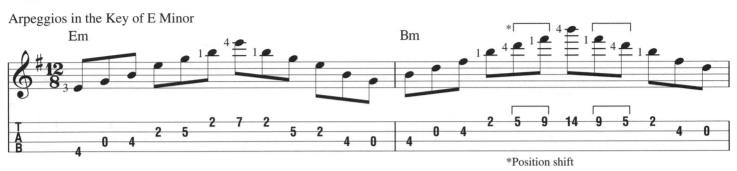

*Position shift

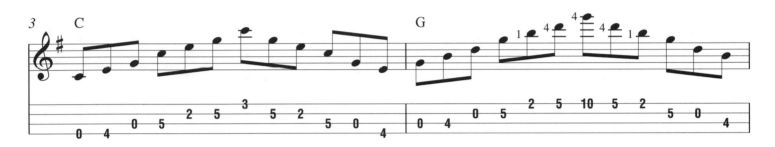

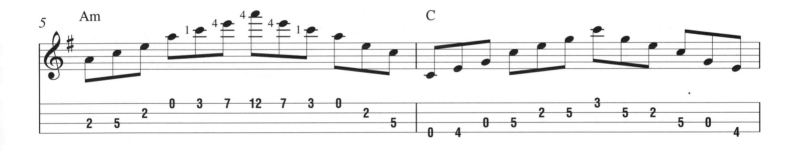

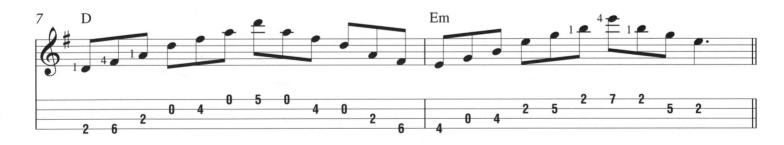

ARPEGGIO SEQUENCE IN THE KEY OF E MINOR

This arpeggio sequence is based on a simple pattern of three consecutive ascending chord tones, with each repetition beginning one chord tone higher than the previous. All the notes are in second position or on open strings except the note (F#) at the fourth string/sixth fret, which you grab with your pinky (thereby extending second position upward by a fret).

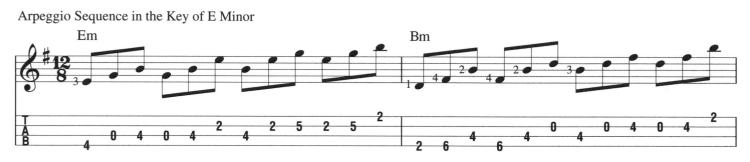

Arpeggio Sequence in the Key of E Minor

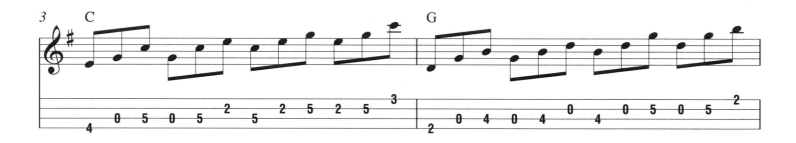

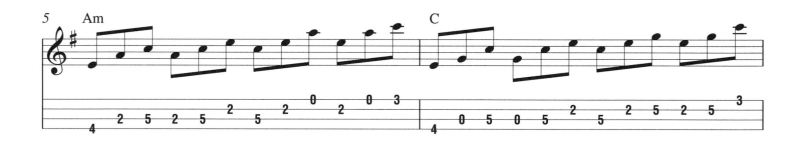

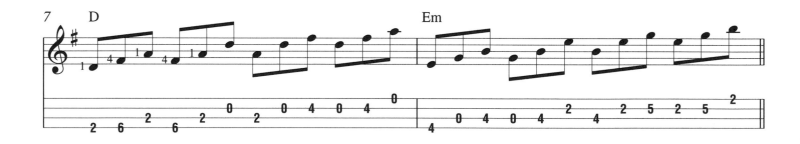

STRUM-AND-SING SONG IN THE KEY OF E MINOR

In the American Civil War song "When Johnny Comes Marching Home," you play two familiar chords (G and D) and three new ones (Em, B, and B7). The B and B7 chords contain a D♯ note, which is derived from the E harmonic minor scale. This "raised 7th" tone (D♯) is seen in the two songs that follow as well.

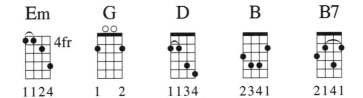 **WHEN JOHNNY COMES MARCHING HOME**

        Em   G   D   B   B7
     [chord diagrams]

        Em   G   D
When Johnny comes marching home again, hurrah, hurrah!

        Em   G   B
We'll give him a hearty welcome then, hurrah, hurrah!

    G   B
The men will cheer, the boys will shout.

    Em   B
The ladies they will all turn out.

       G D Em B   Em   B7   Em
And we'll all feel gay when Johnny comes marching home.

MELODY IN THE KEY OF E MINOR

People have humorously applied the lyrics "Little Mozart is locked in the closet; let him out, let him out, let him out" to the melody of his Symphony No. 40. The original key is G minor, but for the sake of this chapter, we've transposed it to E minor. Watch for the slurs, all of which are pull-offs. The melody falls nicely in second position, with a few temporary moves to first position (as indicated). Again, use a pick and employ alternate picking.

 MOZART'S SYMPHONY NO. 40

SOLO PIECE IN THE KEY OF E MINOR

The American folk song "Wayfaring Stranger" (also called "Poor Wayfaring Stranger" or "I Am a Poor Wayfaring Stranger") has been recorded by numerous folk and country artists, including Joan Baez, Johnny Cash, Emmylou Harris, Burl Ives, and Pete Seeger. The arrangement here is in so-called Carter style, which is named for the playing style of Maybelle Carter of the Carter Family, who were a popular band in the mid-1900s.

In Carter style, you play the melody on the low strings, and in between the melody notes, you strum chords on the high strings. Note the down and up strumming indications in the first full measure: ⊓ = downstroke, and ∨ = upstroke. The indication *sim.* after the strum indications stands for *simile*, which is an instruction telling you to keep strumming in a similar manner (that is, strum down on the downbeats and up on the offbeats).

Carter style is usually played fingerstyle (as Maybelle Carter played), with the thumb playing the low melody and the fingers strumming the chords. But if you prefer, you can use a pick for all the notes. As usual, with solo pieces, allow the melody notes to ring as long as possible (even as you strum chords above them).

Watch for the first and second endings on the repeat. At the last measure of the score, the instruction *D.S. al Fine* (pronounced *FEE-na*y) is Italian and stands for *dal segno* (from the sign) *al fine* (to the place where the music finishes). So, after playing the last measure, go back to the sign (*segno*, which looks like a thick, slanted "S" with a line through it and dots around it) and play to the beat marked *Fine*, skipping over the first ending and taking the second ending instead, as instructed at the final measure. To put it in terms of measure numbers, after playing measure 19, play measures 1–5, then measures 9, 10, and the first beat only of measure 11.

 WAYFARING STRANGER

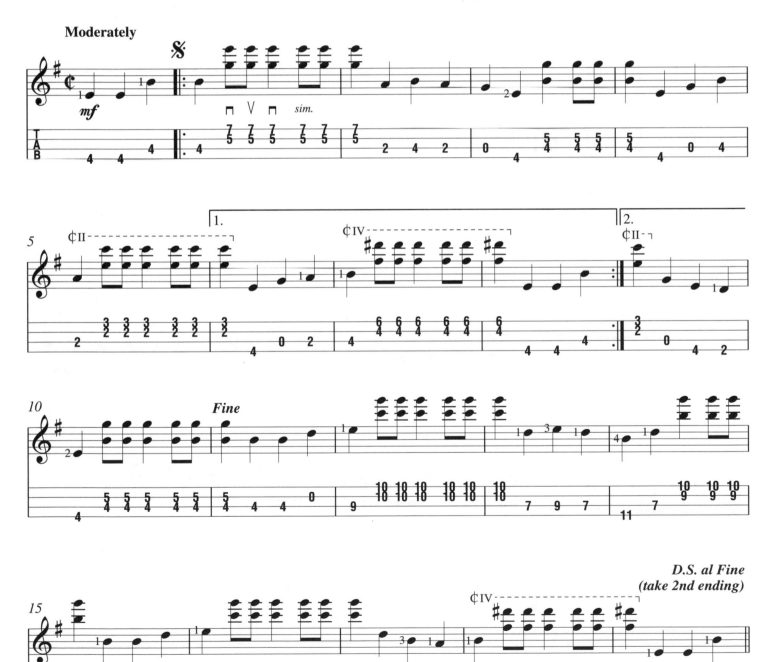

KEY OF D MINOR

The last key we'll cover in this book is D minor.

D MINOR SCALE

The key of D minor is the relative minor of F major and therefore contains the same tones as the F major scale; but, of course, the D minor scale starts from D instead of F. The notes of this scale fall mainly in second position and on open strings, but note that you "extend" second position downward by a fret to grab the Bb note at the first string/first fret with your first finger.

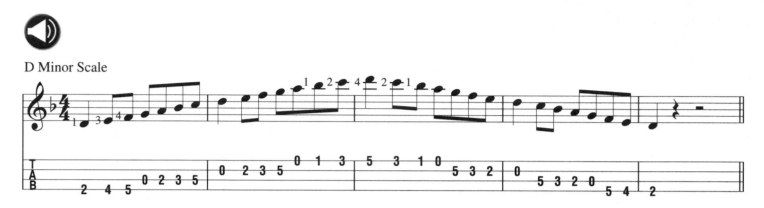

D Minor Scale

D MINOR SCALE SEQUENCE

The pattern of this scale sequence consists of three descending steps followed by an ascending skip of a 3rd (a distance equal to two steps), with each repetition beginning a step higher than the previous. Of course, in the second half of the example (the descending portion), the directions are reversed. The fretted notes fall mainly in second position, but watch for temporary moves out of position when you play notes on the first string.

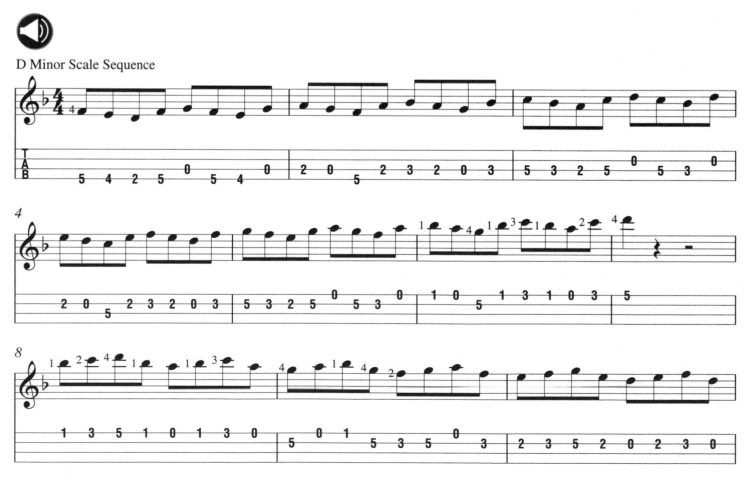

D Minor Scale Sequence

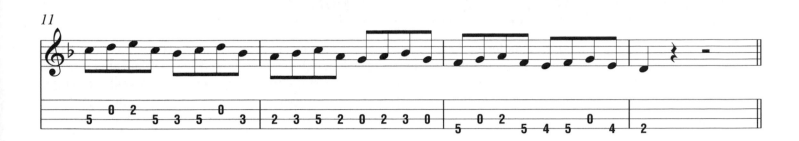

ARPEGGIOS IN THE KEY OF D MINOR

In the key of D minor, the modified minor Pachelbel progression yields the chords Dm, F, Gm, Am, B♭, and C. The arpeggio example below, with its numerous position shifts and its wide range, takes you all over the fretboard—from the first fret all the way up to the 13th.

Arpeggios in the Key of D Minor

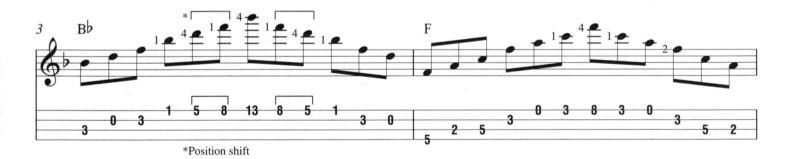

*Position shift

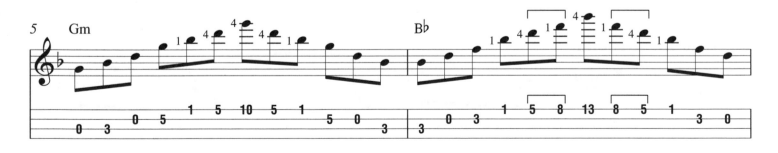

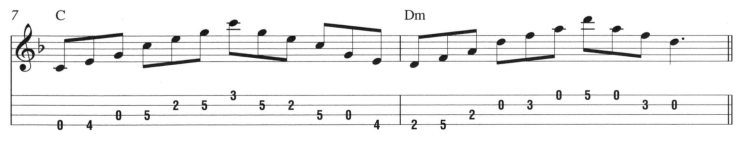

ARPEGGIO SEQUENCE IN THE KEY OF D MINOR

Unlike the previous example, the fretted notes of the arpeggio sequence below fall entirely within second position. Again, watch for two-string barres whenever the same finger plays consecutive notes on adjacent strings at the same fret. The four-note pattern of the sequence consists of an ascent that skips over one chord tone, an ascent to the closest chord tone, and finally a descent to the closest chord tone, with each repetition of the pattern beginning one chord tone higher than the previous.

Arpeggio Sequence in the Key of D Minor

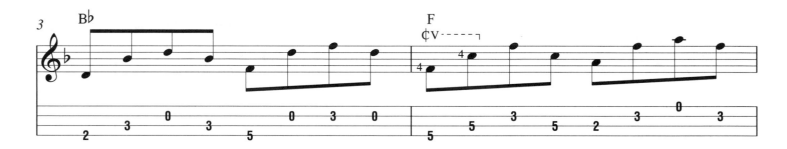

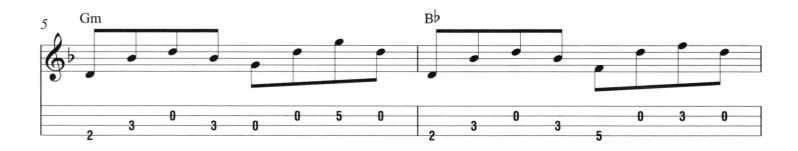

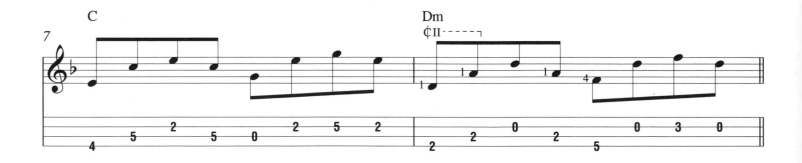

STRUM-AND-SING SONG IN THE KEY OF D MINOR

In the key of D minor, most of the chords of the traditional English folk song "Scarborough Fair" are already familiar to you, but the first chord, Dm, is new. Note that the G chord contains a B note, which is the raised 6th of the D melodic minor scale.

From playing the seven "strum and sing" songs in this book, you've learned more than 20 basic tenor guitar chord fingerings. For additional chords, see "Appendix A: 48 Common Chords." If you need to find the fingering of any chord not covered in this book, do an Internet search for the chord by entering the name of the chord along with the phrase *tenor guitar*. If the chord you're looking for is not found, try using the phrase *tenor banjo* (the fingering for tenor banjo and tenor guitar are the same because they're both tuned C–G–D–A, and so their chord fingerings are the same as well).

If the chord you want is still not found, try using the search term *mandolin* along with the chord name. However, because the mandolin is tuned a 5th higher than the tenor guitar, you need to search for the mandolin chord whose *root* (the note after which the chord is named) is a 5th higher than that of the chord you actually want. For example, if you want, say, a Csus4 chord for tenor banjo, search for Gsus4 for mandolin (because the respective fingerings are the same). And if you need help finding the letter name of the note that's a 5th above any given note, see the fretboard diagram at the top of Appendix B. For any given note in the chart, the note directly above it (on the next higher adjacent string) is a 5th above.

 SCARBOROUGH FAIR

Dm   C   F   G   B♭

1124   13   134   1 2   2341

Dm   C   Dm F   Dm   G   Dm
Are you going to Scarborough Fair? Parsley, sage, rosemary and thyme.

   B♭   F   C   Dm   G   C   Dm
Remember me to the one who lives there, for once she was a true love of mine.

Dm   C   Dm F   Dm   G   Dm
Tell her to make me a cambric shirt. Parsley, sage, rosemary, and thyme.

   B♭   F   C   Dm   G   C   Dm
Without any seam or needlework. Then she shall be a true love of mine.

MELODY IN THE KEY OF D MINOR

Beethoven's lovely "Für Elise" is one of the world's most famous classical piano pieces. The original key is A minor, but for the sake of this chapter, we've transposed it to D minor. The fretted notes fall mainly in second position, but, as shown by the fingerings, you have to "extend" the position upward one fret as you grab the occasional sixth-fret notes with your pinky and downward one fret as you grab the first-fret note (measure 10) with your first finger.

 FÜR ELISE

SOLO PIECE IN THE KEY OF D MINOR

In this arrangement of the traditional English Christmas carol "God Rest Ye Merry, Gentlemen," nearly every melody note is harmonized by a bass note below it, creating a series of double stops. Because the strings involved in the double stops are not always adjacent, use the right-hand fingers, rather than a pick, for this one. Use the thumb for the lower note and either the index or middle finger for the upper note. For the left hand, use any fingering that feels comfortable. Note that, in measure 12, you have an opportunity to play a pull-off to a note that's part of a barre. Make sure your left-hand fingers are holding down both the barre at the second fret and the note at the third fret before you execute the pull-off.

 GOD REST YE MERRY, GENTLEMEN

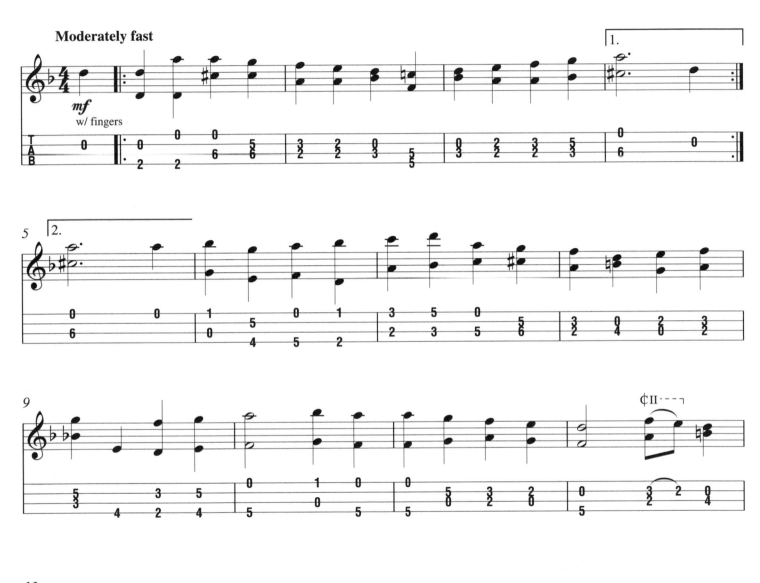

APPENDIX A: 48 COMMON CHORDS

In the "strum and sing" arrangements you play, you learn numerous chords, including all the basic major chords and a variety of minor chords and seventh chords. The chart below provides fingerings for many additional chords. Any chord not included here can likely be found by means of an Internet search, as explained in the "strum and sing" section of the Key of D Minor chapter.

APPENDIX B: NOTES ON THE STAFF

Music readers (or would-be music readers) who want to relate the notes on the fretboard of the tenor guitar to standard music notation can consult the chart below. The fretboard diagram at the top shows the letter name of the note found at each fret of each of the four strings, up to the 12th fret. These notes are reproduced, string by string, in standard notation on the four individual music staves below. (Remember that all notes on the tenor guitar actually sound an octave lower than written!)

For notes above the 12th fret, keep in mind that the letter names are the same as those 12 frets lower; that is, the letter names at the 13th fret are the same as those of the first fret, the letter names at the 14th fret are the same as those of the second, and so on.

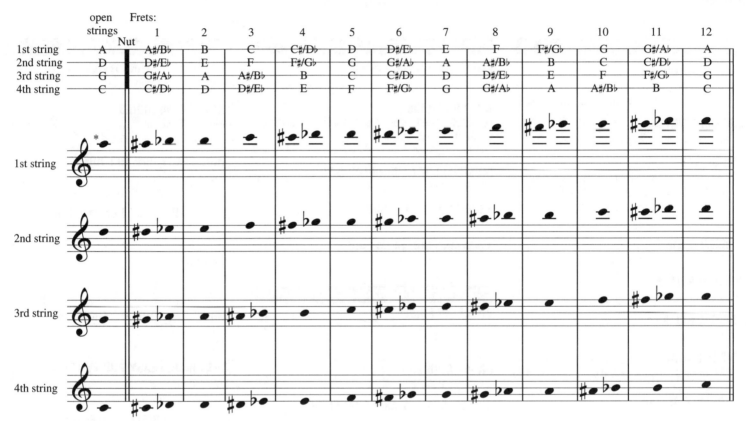

*All notes sound an octave lower than written.

HAL LEONARD GUITAR METHOD

METHOD BOOKS, SONGBOOKS AND REFERENCE BOOKS

THE HAL LEONARD GUITAR METHOD is designed for anyone just learning to play acoustic or electric guitar. It is based on years of teaching guitar students of all ages, and it also reflects some of the best guitar teaching ideas from around the world. This comprehensive method includes: A learning sequence carefully paced with clear instructions; popular songs which increase the incentive to learn to play; versatility – can be used as self-instruction or with a teacher; audio accompaniments so that students have fun and sound great while practicing.

BOOK 1
00699010	Book Only	$9.99
00699027	Book/Online Audio	$14.99
00697341	Book/Online Audio + DVD	$27.99
00697318	DVD Only	$19.99
00155480	Deluxe Beginner Edition (Book, CD, DVD, Online Audio/ Video & Chord Poster)	$22.99

COMPLETE (BOOKS 1, 2 & 3)
00699040	Book Only	$19.99
00697342	Book/Online Audio	$27.99

BOOK 2
00699020	Book Only	$9.99
00697313	Book/Online Audio	$14.99

BOOK 3
00699030	Book Only	$9.99
00697316	Book/Online Audio	$14.99

Prices, contents and availability subject to change without notice.

STYLISTIC METHODS

ACOUSTIC GUITAR
00697347	Method Book/Online Audio	$19.99
00237969	Songbook/Online Audio	$17.99

BLUEGRASS GUITAR
00697405	Method Book/Online Audio	$19.99

BLUES GUITAR
00697326	Method Book/Online Audio (9" x 12")	$16.99
00697344	Method Book/Online Audio (6" x 9")	$15.99
00697385	Songbook/Online Audio (9" x 12")	$16.99
00248636	Kids Method Book/Online Audio	$14.99

BRAZILIAN GUITAR
00697415	Method Book/Online Audio	$17.99

CHRISTIAN GUITAR
00695947	Method Book/Online Audio	$17.99

CLASSICAL GUITAR
00697376	Method Book/Online Audio	$16.99

COUNTRY GUITAR
00697337	Method Book/Online Audio	$24.99

FINGERSTYLE GUITAR
00697378	Method Book/Online Audio	$22.99
00697432	Songbook/Online Audio	$19.99

FLAMENCO GUITAR
00697363	Method Book/Online Audio	$17.99

FOLK GUITAR
00697414	Method Book/Online Audio	$16.99

JAZZ GUITAR
00695359	Book/Online Audio	$22.99
00697386	Songbook/Online Audio	$16.99

JAZZ-ROCK FUSION
00697387	Book/Online Audio	$24.99

R&B GUITAR
00697356	Book/Online Audio	$19.99
00697433	Songbook/CD Pack	$16.99

ROCK GUITAR
00697319	Book/Online Audio	$19.99
00697383	Songbook/Online Audio	$19.99

ROCKABILLY GUITAR
00697407	Book/Online Audio	$19.99

OTHER METHOD BOOKS

BARITONE GUITAR METHOD
00242055	Book/Online Audio	$12.99

GUITAR FOR KIDS
00865003	Method Book 1/Online Audio	$14.99
00697402	Songbook/Online Audio	$12.99
00128437	Method Book 2/Online Audio	$14.99

MUSIC THEORY FOR GUITARISTS
00695790	Book/Online Audio	$22.99

TENOR GUITAR METHOD
00148330	Book/Online Audio	$14.99

12-STRING GUITAR METHOD
00249528	Book/Online Audio	$22.99

METHOD SUPPLEMENTS

ARPEGGIO FINDER
00697352	6" x 9" Edition	$9.99
00697351	9" x 12" Edition	$10.99

BARRE CHORDS
00697406	Book/Online Audio	$16.99

CHORD, SCALE & ARPEGGIO FINDER
00697410	Book Only	$24.99

GUITAR TECHNIQUES
00697389	Book/Online Audio	$16.99

INCREDIBLE CHORD FINDER
00697200	6" x 9" Edition	$7.99
00697208	9" x 12" Edition	$9.99

INCREDIBLE SCALE FINDER
00695568	6" x 9" Edition	$9.99
00695490	9" x 12" Edition	$9.99

LEAD LICKS
00697345	Book/Online Audio	$12.99

RHYTHM RIFFS
00697346	Book/Online Audio	$14.99

SONGBOOKS

CLASSICAL GUITAR PIECES
00697388	Book/Online Audio	$12.99

EASY POP MELODIES
00697281	Book Only	$7.99
00697440	Book/Online Audio	$16.99

(MORE) EASY POP MELODIES
00697280	Book Only	$7.99
00697269	Book/Online Audio	$16.99

(EVEN MORE) EASY POP MELODIES
00699154	Book Only	$7.99
00697439	Book/Online Audio	$16.99

EASY POP RHYTHMS
00697336	Book Only	$10.99
00697441	Book/Online Audio	$16.99

(MORE) EASY POP RHYTHMS
00697338	Book Only	$9.99
00697322	Book/Online Audio	$16.99

(EVEN MORE) EASY POP RHYTHMS
00697340	Book Only	$9.99
00697323	Book/Online Audio	$16.99

EASY POP CHRISTMAS MELODIES
00697417	Book Only	$12.99
00697416	Book/Online Audio	$16.99

EASY POP CHRISTMAS RHYTHMS
00278177	Book Only	$6.99
00278175	Book/Online Audio	$14.99

EASY SOLO GUITAR PIECES
00110407	Book Only	$12.99

REFERENCE

GUITAR PRACTICE PLANNER
00697401	Book Only	$7.99

GUITAR SETUP & MAINTENANCE
00697427	6" x 9" Edition	$16.99
00697421	9" x 12" Edition	$14.99

For more info, songlists, or to purchase these and more books from your favorite music retailer, go to

halleonard.com

HAL•LEONARD®